Discover other cultures

Masks
Around The World

Meryl Doney

D0183029

FRANKLIN WATTS
LONDON•SYDNEY

About this book

In this book you will find examples of masks from around the world. We hope the masks will interest you enough to find out more about them, and will inspire you to make masks of your own. Throughout the book, maps will show you where the different masks come from.

If you are interested in the masks of one particular country, see if you can find other books about that country and learn more about its customs and culture.

We have suggested many different materials and methods for making the masks, to give you a choice. You do not have to follow the same methods that we have used in the book. Decide which technique is best for the mask you want to make.

Most of the steps are very easy to follow, but where you see this sign ask for help from an adult.

Performing plays and stories

If you are making masks as part of a group, you may like to invent a play to perform using the characters you have created. You could also make a series of masks from one country, and then enact a traditional story such as the Krishna legend (see page 10).

Let your imagination run away with you as you make your masks, and have fun wearing them. With a mask, you can be anyone you want to be!

Originally published as World Crafts: Masks

This edition first published in 2002
© Franklin Watts 1995, 2002
Text © Meryl Doney 1995

Franklin Watts
96 Leonard Street, London EC2A 4XD

Franklin Watts Australia
56 O'Riordan Street, Alexandria, NSW 2015

ISBN: 0 7496 4547 4 (pbk)
Dewey Decimal Classification Number 745.5

Series editor: Annabel Martin
Editor: Jane Walker
Design: Visual Image
Cover design: Chloë Cheesman/Mike Davis
Artwork: Ruth Levy
Photography: Peter Millard

With special thanks to Alison Croft, educational advisor and mask maker.

A CIP catalogue record for this book is available from the British Library

Printed in Dubai

Contents

A history of masks

Everybody wants to change the way they look at times. We may change a hairstyle, wear a wig, use face paints or make-up. Perhaps the most dramatic way of changing our appearance is by wearing a mask. Masks make an occasion special too, like Hallowe'en or a birthday party.

Actors use masks to take on a completely new character, but wrestlers wear them to seem more frightening. Children like to pretend to be their favourite character, from Miss Piggy to Spiderman!

Throughout history, masks have been worn, all over the world, for purposes like these. One of the oldest masks, found in South America, is a fossil vertebra of a llama. It was carved into the head of a coyote, and was made sometime between 12,000 and 10,000 years BC. In Africa, the famous Tassili rock paintings in the Sahara region, which were painted some 4,000 years ago, show a similar mask to those made in Zaire and Angola today.

Masks still play an important part in most cultures of the world. They are worn when people want to be serious, funny, clownish, beautiful, frightening or intriguing. Masks still educate and entertain us. They also give us a chance to be someone else for a few moments.

Your own mask-making kit

Put together your own mask-making kit by collecting materials such as plastic bottles, packaging, oddments from jumble sales, beads, badges and novelty gifts. Keep small items in plastic pots, and the rest in a big cardboard box together with a set of tools. Use one of the recipes below to make papier mâché.

Here are some of the most useful items for your mask-making kit:

hammer • tenon saw • hacksaw • coping saw • awl • hand drill • needle-nosed pliers • scissors • craft knife • metal ruler • brushes • white emulsion • poster paints • varnish • PVA (white) glue • tube of strong glue • plastic modelling material • sticky tape • masking tape • card • paper •

tissue paper • newspaper • pen • pencil • felt pens • fabric and felt • needle and thread • decorations, including sequins, braid, tin foil, sticky shapes and beads • newspaper, card and board to work on • apron • paper towels for cleaning up

Papier mâché

petroleum jelly
both pink and white newspaper
PVA glue with a little water added
paint brushes (several sizes)

Apply layer of petroleum jelly if you want to remove papier mâché from the object to be covered.

Tear paper into medium or small pieces, depending on the object you are covering. Cover object evenly with overlapping pieces of paper, painting PVA glue over each piece as you lay it down.

Alternate pink and white newspaper for each layer until you have the correct thickness. For a finer surface, use tissue paper for the top layers.

Other glues, like wallpaper paste and flour and water paste, can also be used.

Papier mâché pulp

paper
PVA glue
1 tablespoon linseed oil
few drops of wintergreen (from chemist)
2 tablespoons wallpaper paste

Tear paper into pieces about 25 mm square. Put in bucket and add water. Soak overnight.

Transfer to large pot with clean water and boil for 20 mins to loosen fibres. When cool, use an electric whisk or blender to pulp paper.

Put pulp in sieve and press with hands to remove water. In bowl, mix pulp with 2 tablespoons PVA glue, linseed oil and wintergreen. Stir thoroughly and sprinkle in the wallpaper paste.

Festival masks

In Mexico, All Saints' Day (1st November) is celebrated as a festival called the Day of the Dead. It is the day when the souls of dead people are believed to return to the world to spend a short time with their relatives.

A wonderful feast is laid out in their honour and all the family members gather together. Far from being an unhappy occasion, the Day of the Dead is a time to enjoy life and the family, to make fun of the authorities and to celebrate death as part of life.

All kinds of decorations and toys are made and sold for these celebrations. There are cut paper pictures, garlands of flowers, pottery figures, and skulls and coffins made from sugar. Skeletons, such as the one shown here, are everywhere, doing everything from dancing to playing football!

There are many dances to celebrate this feast. *Xantolo* dancers go from house to house. The men dress as women and wear masks that are carved from wood. Nahuatl-speaking villagers wear skull and devil masks during *La Danza de los Diablos* (the Dance of the Devils).

Make a Day of the Dead skull

A simple way to make a quick mask is to buy a cheap plastic one. Cover it with a thin layer of papier mâché, and repaint it. Here we have transformed a Hallowe'en mask into a typical Mexican Day of the Dead skull.

This method could also be used to make a horned devil. Form horns from wire covered with newspaper and masking tape. Attach the horns to your mask before the papier mâché stage.

You will need: a pre-formed plastic mask • masking tape • newspaper (pink and white) • PVA glue • white emulsion paint • poster or acrylic paints • glitter • glue • string, Christmas decorations and feathers for hair

2 Paint with white emulsion. When dry, paint and decorate. Add glitter by sprinkling it over patches of glue. Make hair from string, Christmas decorations or feathers.

1 Fix mask firmly to surface with tape. Spread with PVA glue and cover with three layers of newspaper (alternate pink and white layers to show how much you have covered). Allow to dry.

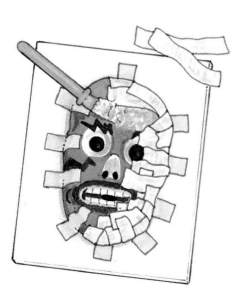

African tradition

The continent of Africa is known for its masks, which play an important role in African life. This is particularly true among the peoples who live south of the Sahara Desert. Within this vast area there are hundreds of groups with different traditions, and their masks are very varied and distinctive. Masks are made from local materials such as wood, raffia, animal skins, bark cloth and cowry shells. Natural paints and dyes are used for decoration, and odd objects like bottle tops and toys are sometimes added.

African masks are used in a variety of ways. They may be worn for important ceremonies, such as a coming of age, a wedding or a funeral, as part of the ritual of secret societies, or to make crops grow or bring rain. They are also used in healing rituals to drive away illness and even to exorcise, or frighten away, evil spirits.

This link with spirits gives masks their powerful impact. Even this wall mask, which was made for tourists and bought in Tunisia, North Africa, has a strong presence.

Make an African wall mask

You will need: strong, corrugated card from supermarket boxes · newspaper for cutting on · PVA glue · strong glue · dark-brown shoe polish · old rag and toothbrush

1 Draw a rough sketch of the mask you want to make. Mark out basic shape on card. Lay card on newspaper and cut out shape with a craft knife (always cut away from your fingers).

2 Use shape to mark out second piece of card. Cut out mask 1 cm smaller than first one. Glue second shape to first. Repeat this step again to build up mask shape. Add face shape.

3 Cut the following pieces for the face: 5 nose, 6 eye, 2 mouth, 2 teeth, 2 bird-shaped and several smaller pieces. Stick some pieces on flat and some at right angles to build up the face and head.

4 Decorate mask. To make it look like wood, rub with shoe polish.

This mask has been built up from layers of thick corrugated card. It has been painted and polished to look like wood. You could decorate your mask in bright colours with anything that adds impact, such as shells, pasta shapes, seeds and tin foil.

The Krishna legend

Replica masks are sometimes made as decorations or as reminders of a favourite play or performance. These small masks from Orissa, India, are copies of the full-sized masks worn in the *Chhau* dance-drama tradition. The dancers mime traditional Hindu stories. The masks shown here represent characters from the Krishna legend. Some characters are half-man, half-woman or half-demon. The men have moustaches, the women wear nose rings and the demons have long tongues.

The life-sized masks used to be carved from wood, but now they are made from papier mâché. Their wonderful head-dresses are built up from sponge, wood and paper, and decorated with mirrors, beads and tin foil.

Make a replica mask

You will need: small mask (borrowed or bought – try a charity shop or an Indian craft shop) · petroleum jelly · talcum powder · plastic modelling material · plaster of Paris · water · loop of wire · poster paints · varnish

This is a method to make a copy of a mask as a wall decoration or gift. Once you have made the mould you can make as many masks as you like, and decorate each one differently.

1 Smooth petroleum jelly over mask and dust with talcum powder. Roll out plastic modelling material thickly and press onto mask. Trim off excess.

2 Gently ease modelling material off mask and turn it upside down. Rest on a pad of modelling material without damaging the shape.

3 Mix up plaster of Paris until it is as thick as double cream. Pour into mould until full.

Push loop of wire into wet plaster. Leave to dry.

4 Ease plastic modelling material off plaster mask. (If you want to use mould again, press it back onto original mask to renew shape.) Paint and varnish the new mask. You can decorate it with sequins, beads, etc.

Acting in masks

The use of masks in Europe can be traced back to the Greek theatre. All actors in Greek plays wore masks to express their characters, which were either good or evil. The early Greek plays were often performed in mime. The mime tradition was revived in Italy in the fourteenth century, when travelling groups of players performed comedies featuring well-known masked characters: Pantalone, a miserly merchant (shown above); Coveillo, a musician; Pulcinello (who became the basis of the Mr Punch character); and Arlecchino (Harlequin), the childlike, lovesick acrobat.

All these characters wore traditional masks and costumes. They were known and loved throughout Europe, and their theatre style was called *commedia dell'arte*.

Make a *commedia dell'arte* mask

This mask is fun to make because it is moulded directly from the face. It will therefore only fit one person. It is made with plaster-soaked bandage. Make this by cutting short strips of medical bandage or plasterers' scrim and dipping them into a thick mixture of plaster of Paris. Alternatively, dry plaster bandage can be bought from craft shops. It is sometimes called Mod-Roc.

You will need: someone to act as your model (if you want the mask for yourself, ask someone to apply the plaster to your face) • apron and hair band • newspaper • petroleum jelly • strips of bandage or dry plaster bandage • plaster of Paris • white emulsion and poster paints • varnish • ribbon to tie mask to head • papier mâché pulp • glue

1 Prepare model: fasten back hair, cover with protective apron and lay on table covered with newspaper. Smooth petroleum jelly over upper face, especially eyebrows and hairline. Leave eyes and nostrils free.

2 Mix plaster to a thick cream. Dip bandages and lay on face until whole mask area is covered. Add two more layers. Leave for 5 minutes until hard. (If using dry plaster bandage, follow instructions.)

3 Gently ease dry mask away from face. If you want a smooth mask, paint with white emulsion. Paint, decorate and varnish mask. Make holes at sides to attach ribbons.

4 To make Pantalone or other *commedia dell'arte* characters, make features from papier mâché pulp glued to the mask. Allow to dry before painting. Pantalone is painted white, then with a grey wash to age him.

Nō theatre masks

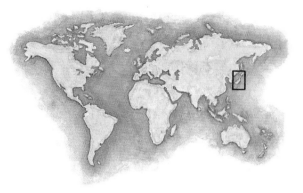

The best-known form of Japanese theatre is called *Nō*. Its plays grew from early religious festivals concerned with planting and harvest, combined with the folk plays of travelling Chinese actors, jugglers and acrobats. The simplicity and classic style of *Nō* theatre are based on the principles of Zen Buddhism. The ideas of *yugen*, or grace, darkness and mystery are very important.

All the roles in *Nō* are played by men, who undergo a long training in the art. The masks are small and tied to the head, covering only the front of the face. Each mask has a serene, neutral expression, and traditionally the actor must not change his voice. He must bring the character to life through subtle movements of his body.

This mask is Waka Onna, a young girl who appears in the play *Dojoji*.

Make a *Nō* character

You will need: round balloon · shoe box · petroleum jelly · materials for papier mâché · tissue paper · newspaper · PVA glue · plaster of Paris and water · sponge · fine sandpaper · wire wool · white emulsion and poster paints · varnish

Nō masks are traditionally very smooth. To achieve this effect, cover the mask with a plaster mixture before painting. (For a harder surface you can use gesso, a mixture of chalk and rabbit-skin size. This can be bought, ready made, from craft shops.) If you would like to make other *Nō* characters, look them up in a book on Japanese arts.

2 Draw face on mask. Build up features with glued newspaper and tissue paper. Add three more layers of tissue paper papier mâché. Allow to dry.

1 Blow up and tie balloon. Wedge into shoe box to form oval face-shape. Cover top surface with petroleum jelly. Add three layers of papier mâché. Allow to dry.

3 Ease mask off balloon. Neaten edges and strengthen with more papier mâché. Paint mask with thick plaster mixture and PVA glue. When dry, smooth with wire wool. Paint with emulsion. Sand, paint and varnish.

PAPUA NEW GUINEA

Bush and sea spirits

In Papua New Guinea, people used to belong to large clans, which were organised by secret societies of the senior men. The seniors were responsible for marking important events in the life of the clan with complicated rituals. These rituals involved special masks which were often huge. They were made of bark cloth and cane, with leaf skirts, so that they were light enough for people to wear.

The western Elema people performed long ceremonies or ritual cycles. This mask represents the *Kovave*, or bush spirits, and was used for the initiation of boys who were ready to become adults.

16

Make a *Kovave* mask

This mask is designed to make the person wearing it look very tall and menacing. It is worn on top of the head and the skirt completely hides the wearer's face.

You will need: plastic bottle • masking tape • cardboard tube (from roll of tin foil) • rectangular ice-cream tub • materials for papier mâché • cotton fabric • stiff card • strong glue • white emulsion and poster paints • raffia • brown wrapping paper, 100 x 100 cm

1 Cut off base of bottle. Fit tube over neck and tape. Cover with three layers of papier mâché. Allow to dry. Glue to ice-cream tub with cotton fabric strip cut into tabs.

2 Cover entire mask with three more layers of papier mâché. Allow to dry. Cut 2 beaks and 2 side pieces from stiff card. Glue these to the bottle.

3 Paint whole mask with emulsion. Paint and decorate. (Paint ice-cream tub base brown.) Add tufts of raffia to side pieces and at top.

4 Fold brown paper in half and cut into narrow strip fringe.

5 Wrap and glue fringe around base of bottle. Glue on more raffia to add to skirt.

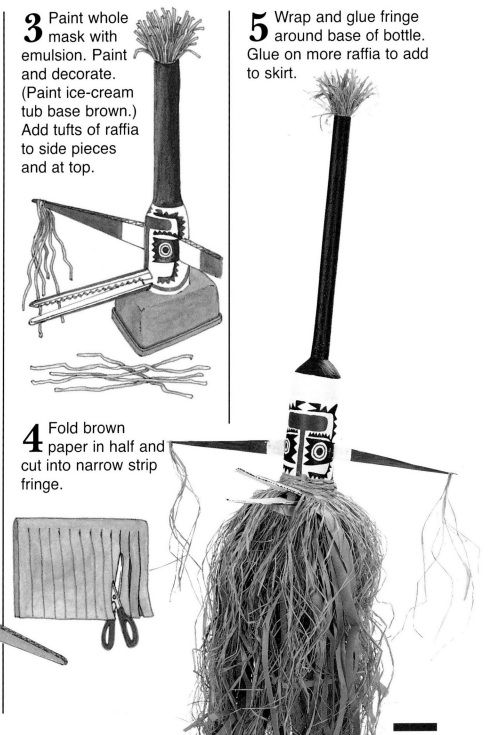

'Curing' masks

This small
wooden mask is a
replica of a Sri Lankan
Sanni, or 'curing', mask. These
masks are worn in ritual healing
ceremonies called *Sanni Yakuma*. According
to tradition, evil spirits cause different illnesses.
Therefore, when the spirit of a disease sees the masked
'spirit' dancing, it is driven out of the sick person who
can then recover.

There are about eighteen different masks, each one
representing a spirit such as fever, shivering or vomiting.
The colour of the masks is very important. For example,
the spirit of vomiting is coloured blue, and demons are
painted in reds and greens.

Make a wooden *Sanni* mask

This small replica mask has been carved from hardwood. It is very simple and worth experimenting with if you have never carved before. For the full-sized version you need to use a softer wood such as balsa, or a different method altogether, such as papier mâché or clay.

You will need: 3-cm dowelling, 10 cm long • sharp 6-mm chise • mallet • sandpaper and sandsticks • thin plywood or balsa wood, 5 x 10 cm • glue • wire tack • white emulsion and poster paints • varnish • white card • 2 black mapping pins

1 Draw simple face on dowel. Grip in vice and chisel out the shape, front and back. (Always work away from yourself, turning dowel when necessary. If important bits chip off, glue them back on immediately and wait until glue dries before continuing.)

Chip off back of dowel until it is flat. Hollow out small area at the top.

2 Draw shape of side pieces, with tabs, on paper. Cut out. Use as pattern to draw two shapes on plywood or balsa. Cut out with coping saw or craft knife. Smooth wood on both sides. Paint all pieces with emulsion.

3 Glue tabs onto back of dowel. Attach a wire tack to hang up your mask. Decorate with poster paint. Varnish. For eyes, cut out card circles. Push mapping pins through card and into mask.

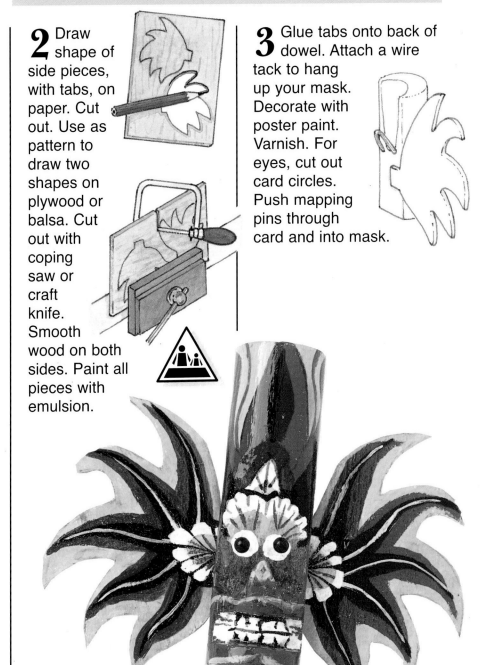

Sanding hint: A sandstick is very useful for smoothing awkward corners after carving. Spread glue on a length of the smallest diameter half-dowel and wrap fine sandpaper around it.

Aztec masks

This small replica mask was made in Mexico City, where one family specialises in making things from recycled metal. It is based on the rich mask-making tradition of the Aztec peoples of Mexico. Masks in this early civilisation were made from semi-precious stones like jade, obsidian and turquoise, and from metals such as copper, silver and gold.

Masks were used in a variety of ways. Images of the gods were made to cover the faces of the dead. Warriors wore head-dresses representing military emblems, such as the eagle and the jaguar. Even human skulls, from prisoners of war, were used as the basis for highly decorated skull masks.

Make a recycled metal face

This small replica mask has been made from a tin can. This metal is a little difficult to work with, so a large metal mask could be made from a foil pie tin, using the same method.

1 Remove top and bottom of can with opener. Use tin snips to cut tin open. Beat it flat on board with mallet. Draw mask shape with felt pen. Draw line 1 cm round outside of shape.

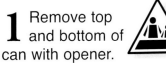

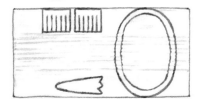

Draw nose and other decorations.

2 Cut out mask and decorations with tin snips. (Pie tin can be cut with scissors.) Snip tin around edge at 1-cm intervals. Fold tin tabs behind mask. (Beware of sharp edges.)

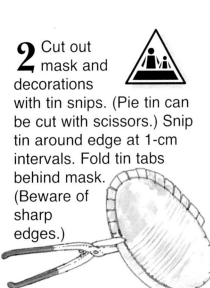

3 Mark features on face. Put mask on polystyrene block and punch holes for eyes and mouth with awl.

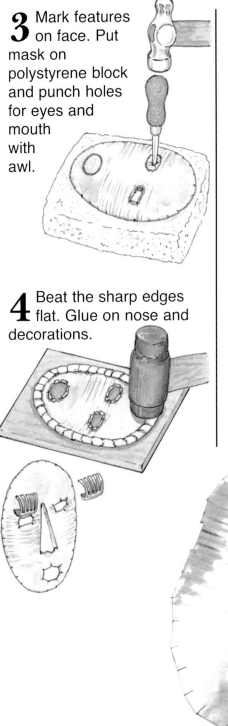

4 Beat the sharp edges flat. Glue on nose and decorations.

5 Draw around mask on felt. Mark eyes and mouth. Cut out mask, eyes and mouth. Glue felt to back to neaten sharp edges. Glue on wire loop.

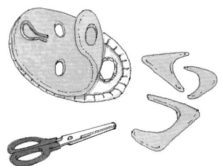

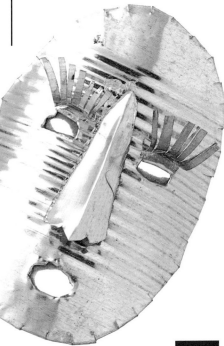

Rain-making and coming of age

Every year in early June, villagers in the Andes mountains of Ecuador celebrate the feast of Corpus Christi with masked dances. These dances may have come from old Inca ceremonies in which people prayed for rain to make their corn grow. The dancers wear colourful clothes and masks such as the one shown on the left. Some of the dancers play noisy, acrobatic devils, while others represent angels or the old Inca star gods. Drummers provide the rhythm of the dances.

Animal masks, like this puma from Peru, were worn for the ceremony to welcome the sons of rich families into manhood. The jaguar and the puma represented the Incas' ancestors who were present at the feast.

Make an Andean mask

In the Andes mountains of South America, masks are made from clay, wood, painted felt or wire mesh. This mask can be made of clay and then biscuit fired if you have access to a kiln. Alternatively you can use self-hardening craft clay. You can make this mask to wear or to hang as a wall decoration.

You will need: newspaper • card • masking tape • clay • rolling pin and board • sponge • white emulsion and poster paints • varnish • string

3 Add more clay to form face or animal features.

4 Remove mask from mould. Smooth front and back with a wet sponge. Biscuit fire or leave to dry hard. Paint mask with white emulsion, decorate and varnish. Attach string to holes.

1 Form crumpled newspaper into a face shape. Stick to card with masking tape.

Leave until half dry. Pierce string holes in the sides if you want to wear the mask, or in the top to hang it. If required, cut out eye holes.

2 Knead clay and roll into oval. Lay over paper mould and smooth shape.

23

PACIFIC ISLANDS

Natural decoration

The islands of Melanesia in the southern Pacific Ocean are famous for their wonderful, varied masks. They are usually produced as part of the elaborate rituals of secret societies. Men are the chief mask-makers and performers, even though some masks represent female spirits.

The masks are often very large, covering the whole head and sometimes the body of the wearer. Melanesian masks are made of natural, local materials such as wood, bark, leather, vegetable fibres and even human hair. They are decorated with cowry, coconut and pearl shells, seeds and feathers. The colours tend to be red, green, black and white because they also have to be produced from local ingredients.

This is a copy of a bird mask, which is worn on the head, rather like a hat. It is from the island of New Britain, Papua New Guinea.

Make a bird mask

The islanders of New Britain use all kinds of local materials to make their masks. Here is a method to make the one shown below. However, you could invent your own method, using anything you have in the house, from string to onion bags, feather dusters or even Christmas tree ornaments!

You will need: old-fashioned, stuffed tea cosy, or material to make one • needle and thread • fabrics: hessian, felt, chamois leather, blanket, sheeting, dishcloth, duster • glue • 25-mm-thick balsa wood • sandpaper • paints • thick coathanger wire (straightened) • polystyrene block • newspaper • jute string (unravelled) • decorations: feathers, toys, beads, buttons, cut-out shapes • raffia

1 Take (or make) tea cosy. Shape and sew top into oval. Sew shaped and torn fabric to hang down and cover completely.

2 Cut and glue on felt animals or shapes. String beads and sew on. Add feathers and other decorations.

3 Draw beak (this one has a bird on it) on both sides of balsa wood. Draw two eyes.

Carve out shapes with craft knife. Sand smooth and paint.

4 Bend wire in half, push through polystyrene and mask. Pack newspaper inside to hold wire and make mask comfortable to wear.

5 Staple and glue beak and eyes to fabric. Wrap raffia around wire. Bind on bunches of string. Sew string crest to top of head.

Animals and ancestors

The Yoruba peoples of south-western Nigeria use masks in their secret ceremonies. This one belongs to the Egungun cult. The spirits of the cult's ancestors are represented by human figures, animals, birds and snakes. The masks are particularly brought out in times of crisis or war, when the ancestors' help is needed.

The mask is carved from one piece of wood. It is usually worn slanting down over the face so that the wearer can look through the eyeholes. These masks can weigh over 25 kilograms. The holes around the edge are made with a hot iron rod and are used for attaching the costume that goes with the mask. The costume is often designed to cover the wearer's whole body.

Make a Yoruba ancestor mask

It would take a very experienced carver to make this mask from a single piece of wood. Here is a simple method that looks just like the original but is very light to wear.

You will need: small-gauge chicken wire, 70 x 80 cm • wire cutters • masking tape • PVA glue • tissue paper and newspaper • wire • white emulsion paint • poster paints in earth colours • thick felt or upholstery lining material

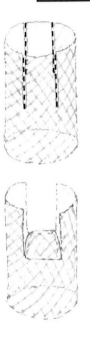

1 Bend chicken wire into tube 70 cm tall. (Use garden gloves and pliers to protect hands.) Make four cuts downwards as shown. Fold middle sections over, 25 cm from bottom, to form head shape.

2 Roll side sections into horns. Bend sharp ends of wire inwards to hold in place. Cut a small section of spare wire to form into a nose. Attach it to mask by bending wire ends.

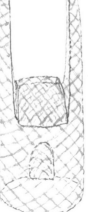

3 Wind tape around at intervals. Cover with tissue paper and PVA glue. Add three layers of papier mâché. Allow to dry.

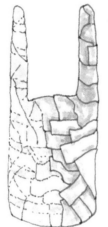

4 Form features and decorations from paper and tape. Make shapes of ancestor spirits in wire. Cover with newspaper and tape and three layers of papier mâché. Allow to dry.

5 Paint with emulsion and poster paints. Do not varnish. Glue decorations to mask. Flatten sharp edges inside and glue in felt lining. Pierce eye and nostril holes. Pad inside with newspaper to make comfortable.

Dragons at New Year

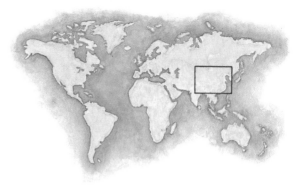

All over the world Chinese communities celebrate their New Year in February, with fireworks and paper dragons winding and dancing through the streets. The dragons have large mask-like heads and bodies that are many metres long. They are made from paper and cane strips, and each one is designed to be carried by a team of around twenty dancers. The dragons are often painted red, which is a symbol of good luck. The colour red is also used for the envelopes of lucky money which are given to children at New Year.

In Chinese folklore, dragons usually bring good fortune. If you have a secret hoard of treasure you can get the treasure dragons to guard it for you.

Make a paper dragon

This is a good mask to make for a lot of people. You can make it as big and as long as you like, adding extra hoops and crêpe paper depending on how many people will be dancing. You will need to practise dancing together so that you do not tear the paper.

You will need: strong cardboard box · 2 split pins/brass fasteners · parcel tape · poster paints · 2 large sheets white card · 4 packs of crêpe paper · tinsel and lametta · 1 table tennis ball

1 Cut off a corner from open end of box. Fix corner back on at an angle with split pins and bind round with sticky tape. Cut out and paint or cover tongue. Make tabs on back of tongue and fix inside box with parcel tape.

2 Cut a piece of card a little shorter than the box but 30 cm wider. Bend this over top and fix with parcel tape. Repeat across back of the head. Cover head (except for jaw) with crêpe paper fixed with parcel tape.

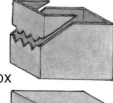

3 Cut out and fold two eye shapes as shown. Staple at the bottom. Loosely fold two 50-cm lengths of tinsel and staple one inside each eye. Cut table tennis ball in half and glue one to each eye. Glue eyes to head.

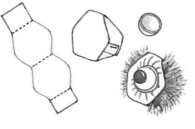

4 For nose and teeth, cut out card and decorate. Glue to front of box. Decorate head with tinsel and lametta fixed with parcel tape and staples.

5 Cut double the number of strips of stiff card (6 x 75 cm) that you need. Staple together in pairs. Cut 80-cm lengths of yellow and green crêpe paper. Staple alternate yellow and green crêpe to the card strips.

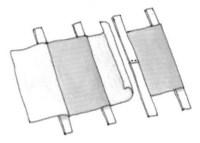

6 Fix front of body inside head with parcel tape. Add fringed crêpe to end. One person holds the dragon's head above his or her head. The others hold card strips.

Useful information

United Kingdom

Some helpful addresses

Barnet Multicultural Study Centre
Barnet Teachers' Centre
451 High Road
Finchley
LONDON N12 0AS

Japan Information and
Cultural Centre
101–104 Piccadilly
LONDON W1V 9FN

Equipment and materials

Hobby Stores
39 Parkway
LONDON NW1
(balsa wood and craft equipment)

Museums

The Museum of Mankind
6 Burlington Gardens
Piccadilly
LONDON W1

Pitt Rivers Museum
University of Oxford
Parks Road
OXFORD

Masks for sale

Centaur Gallery
82 Highgate High Street
LONDON N6
(antique masks)

Jackson Contra-Banned
Unit 2, Gatehouse Enterprise
Centre, Albert Street, Lockwood
HUDDERSFIELD HD1 3QD
*(mail order catalogue and
education packs)*

Joliba
47 Colston Street
BRISTOL BS1 5AX
(West African goods)

Soma Books Ltd
38 Kennington Lane
LONDON SE11 4LS
(Indian craft and book list)

Books

*The Art and Craft of
Papier Mâché*
Juliet Bawden (Mitchell Beazley)

Art of the World series, (Methuen)

Arts & Crafts of South America
Lucy Davies & Mo Fini (Tumi)

Ethnic Sculpture
Malcolm McLeod & John Mack
(British Museum)

Exploring Indian Crafts
Manju Gregory
(Mantra Publishing Ltd)

Handcrafts of India
Kamaladevi Chattopadhyay
(Indian Council for Cultural
Relations)

How to Start Carving
Charles Graveney (Studio Vista)

Make a Mask
Joan Peters & Anna Sutcliffe
(Batsford)

Making Crazy Faces and Masks
Jen Green (Watts Books)

Masks
John Mack
(British Museum Press)

Masks
Lyndie Wright (Watts Books)

Monsters and Masks
Chester Jay Alkema
(Oak Tree Press)

Rainy Days: Masks
Denny Robson (Watts Books)

The Skeleton at the Feast
Elizabeth Carmichael &
Chloë Sayer
(British Museum Press)

Sticky Fingers: Masks
Ting and Neil Morris
(Watts Books)

*Traditions Around the
World: Masks*
Amanda Earl & Danielle Sensier
(Wayland)

*World of Other Faces:
Indian Masks*
Jiwan Pani (Ministry of
Information & Broadcasting, India)

Australia

Progress Amusement
1 Station Street
Malvern Victoria 3166
phone: 03 500 0455
(hobby shop)

Queensland Museum
cm Grey and Melbourne Street
South Brisbane
Queensland 4101
phone: 07 840 7555
(Australian Aboriginal masks)

Aboriginal Art Centre
117 George Street The Rocks
Sydney NSW 2000
phone: 02 247 9625
(masks for sale)

Asian and primative Art Gallery
43 William Street
Paddington NSW
phone: 02 331 7073
(masks for sale and gallery)

Tribal Art Gallery
103 Flinders Lane
Melbourne Victoria
phone: 03 650 4186
(masks for sale and gallery)

Asian Connection Gallery
6 Edmonstone Street
South Brisbane
Queensland 4101
phone: 07 844 0566

Glossary

All Saints' Day November 1st. A Christian celebration of the saints' lives.

Andes A range of mountains which runs down the west coast of South America.

Aztecs People who lived in Mexico AD 1200–1500.

balsa Very soft, light wood from the balsa tree.

biscuit fire To bake clay until it is porous.

cane A long, thin stem of giant reed or grass.

chamois leather Soft leather from sheep, goats or deer.

Corpus Christi The Christian feast which celebrates the Body of Christ.

cowry A sea snail.

cult A group which is formed for religious worship.

emblem A badge or symbol belonging to a person or group.

exorcise To free someone from an evil spirit.

folklore People's traditional beliefs.

Hallowe'en October 31st. The name is a shortened form of All Hallows' Eve, the day before All Saints' Day.

hessian Rough fabric used in furniture making.

Incas The people of Peru who lived there before the Spanish conquered them.

initiation The act of introducing someone to a position or a secret.

jute Bark fibre which is used to make mats and sacking.

kiln An oven for baking, or firing, clay.

Krishna Hindu god and reincarnation of the preserver God, Vishnu.

lucky money Pretend money which is given to children at the Chinese New Year.

Nō A style of Japanese theatre.

raffia Palm-tree fibre which is used to tie plants and to make hats and baskets.

replica An exact model of something.

ritual A religious or solemn series of actions.

semi-precious stone A stone which is less valuable than precious stones like sapphires or diamonds.

upholstery Textile which is used to cover furniture.

yugen An idea from Zen Buddhism which expresses the sense of mystery that masks can bring to a play.

Zen Buddhism A Japanese form of Buddhism.

Index

Additional photographs:

p6, The Hutchison Library © Liba Taylor; p14, Japan Information and Cultural Centre, London; p16 and p26, British Museum; p28, Robert Harding Picture Library.

The bird mask shown on p24 was made by Zoe Neeves.